Walter van Laack

Lectures & Insights

Dying and Death from a Scientific Point Of View

Author

Prof. Dr. med. Walter van Laack
Specialist for Orthopaedics & Orthopaedic Surgery, Physiotherapy, Sports Medicine, Chiropractic and Acupuncture.
Author of numerous books for existential and natural philosophy

Cover

Designed by my son **Martin van Laack, M.A.**
Master of Science in Architecture (RWTH-Aachen)

Translation

by Anneliese Wolstenholme, Roetgen/Germany

© **2018** by **Prof. Dr. Walter van Laack**
van Laack Book Publishers, Aachen (Germany)
www.vanLaack-Buch.de   -   www.vanLaack-Book.eu
www.Nahtoderfahrung.info - www.Near-Death-Experience.net

Printing & distribution by Book-on-Demand (BoD)
In de Tarpen 42, D-22848 Norderstedt (Germany); Fax +49-40-53433584
info@bod.de - www.bod.de

ISBN 978-3-936624-41-0

Dying and Death from a Scientific Point of View

Based on a lecture given by Prof. Dr. med. Walter van Laack,
on 2nd June 2018 in Fulda (Germany)

The famous philosophers Socrates and Plato already assumed that our death must not necessarily mean the end of our existence. On the contrary, they both strongly suggested that we indeed survive this obscure boundary which for us appears to be so impenetrable. They did agree, however, that neither religions nor philosophy will ever be able to give plausible answers to this question, as did Immanuel Kant who arrived at the same conclusion two thousand years later. Religion as well as philosophy could at best come up with some suggestions which sometimes might even sound convincing.

In pursuit of the truth it is, of course, absolutely imperative today to take scientific knowledge into consideration, which includes, among others, also medical knowledge. However, this knowledge, if considered alone and in isolation, is again misleading, unless we explicitly strive for a holistic approach, while thinking out of the box and consistently looking for the proverbial "red thread" which could be suitable as guideline and which should keep leading us back to the "right path" in all our phantasy and philosophy.

However, is there a "red thread" at all? I would think so and in my lecture I try again to explain this in a sustainable and convincing way.

It is a fact that no scientific know-ledge, no measurement and no observation remains completely without interpretation. Everything and anything is usually subject to interpretation within a short time. This interpretation, however, is all too often taken on its own without considering other phenomena and observations which possibly occur in parallel in other areas of scientific knowledge and findings. Besides these findings are always influenced by the current *zeitgeist* which today is, unfortunately, still of *materialistic* nature and thus reduces all interpretations to this basis. Therefore, we talk of *reductionism*. And hence the following applies, a statement which from a scientific and medical point of view is the clearly and uncompromisingly accepted conclusion, widely disseminated by mostly ignorant media: *Our death is definitely the end of our personality.* Or, as the English physicist *Steven Hawking*, who is so highly acclaimed everywhere and who died this year, once said some years ago in an interview: *"I regard the brain as a computer which will stop working when its components fail. There is no heaven or afterlife for broken down computers." ("Welt am Sonntag" 22.05.2011)*

On the other hand, however, there are countless testimonies from a large number of people on earth – and this does not mean just people living today but includes human beings since the beginning of mankind – based on which all kinds of visions and descriptions could lead to a huge wealth and diversity of different and often even contradictory possibilities, as to how we could indeed survive what we call our own death.

Of course, there is always an unbelievable amount of phantasy involved, although in just a few cases this is paired with verifiable experiences which should definitely give us plenty to think about.

This includes, for example, incidents which occur during a so-called "near-death experience" (NDE), which can happen to people involved in an accident or lying on an operating table while being unconscious and undergoing a resuscitation. Sometimes the perceived turns out later to be correct, although this experience could in fact not have been perceived in an extreme and life-threatening situation. It occurred at this special moment outside the respective range of experiences or horizon of knowledge.

This also includes experiences which occur while someone is in a certain alert state of mind: Some people, when in a trance or under hypnosis, seem not only to relive earlier situations of their lives which remain hidden from their normal consciousness or which are possibly suppressed. In some cases they seem to report experiences from previous lives. Sometimes they even speak in a foreign language which they have never learned but which proves to be correct.

In most cases it is impossible to verify the accuracy of such reports. Therefore, from a scientific point of view, these visions or stories must be considered as being pure anecdotes. This does not at all mean that they are pure fiction, but from a scientific point of view they serve no purpose. The same applies to all other similar cases, i.e. on the one hand, to the large group of spontaneous extraordinary experiences of consciousness (EEC), which include near-death experiences (NDE) as a small subgroup. On the other hand, this applies also to people who under hypnosis talk about a possible previous life. Such visions and experiences especially are often classified as true stories from a "previous life". The current life is then interpreted as "carnal rebirth". For this phenomenon the term *"reincarnation"* was first coined 1857 by the French spiritualist *Allan Kardec (1804-1861)*. Today, many hypnotherapists offer so-called "past-life regressions" under hypnosis. Many other researchers believe that they are able to provide scientific evidence to support the belief in reincarnation mostly based on children's visions and reports about verifiable life situations of dead people.

In principle two utterly contrary worlds of imagination clash here: the followers of one camp, due to its apparently "strictly scientific" perception, retreat into their shell of proverbial indifference. However, I think they see the world far too biased and, therefore, reductionistic, i.e. purely materialistic. In the other camp we find a myriad of people who rely solely on their own wealth of experience or that of others, since they aspire to attach more importance to these experiences than to scientific findings, for whatever reasons. Often, this leads to a quite arbitrary potpourri which is rather confusing and difficult to classify. This camp unites many adherents of all institutionalised religions and from the whole range of the so-called esoteric spectrum. In the best case, these groups co-exist, mostly peacefully although with much mutual disdain. Sometimes, unfortunately to an increasing degree at present, in some of these groups the disputes escalate into inacceptable and often violent conflicts, as the actions of many religious fanatics quite painfully demonstrate nowadays.

A survey in Germany in January 2017 among people over 18 years of age illustrates clearly the aforementioned: approximately half of them did not believe that there is a soul, a god, resurrection from the dead, reincarnation, etc., while the other half believed just that although extremely split into factions with very diverse concepts. This survey showed that women are distinctly more "religious" than men, two thirds of whom dismiss everything spiritual *(Statista 2018, 1020 participants)*.

Classical scientists must be reproached for closing their eyes even if something inexplicable can actually be *proven*, although it cannot be reproduced as in the laboratory. In such cases it is mostly ignored or interpreted in a fanciful manner or one refers to the possibility that what is still inexplicable today may be explicable in the future in a reductionist manner. Modern results in the context of near-death research, carried out experimentally in animals and also arbitrarily established, in concurrent observations on dying humans, show exactly that: people will always try to straighten any "curvature" in such a way that it seems to fit into the usual reductionist frame. Even outrageous and conceited interpretations are often not beneath their dignity.

Unfortunately, it is hardly possible to talk to religious fanatics. In some cases this grows into a serious social problem. Only competent politicians, though few and far between nowadays, could solve this problem with reason and foresight through appropriate laws and pragmatic jurisprudence.

Esoterics on the other hand should always be encouraged to pay more attention to "real science". They tend to view many issues notoriously through their once aligned spectacles, whereby they often believe that this perspective is scientifically supported. However, this is often not the case. In my experience over the last decades it is like this: very often pure dogma is paramount here and preconceived opinions diversify in wide variation and in a broad spectrum but without real substance.

After decades of research and intensive study of the issue of death, the question of its finality and the prevalent answers to it from all sciences involved I have come to the following conclusions:

The classical sciences do not always really help here since they usually only deal with the phenomena of their own subject areas and hardly ever look beyond their own horizon and often even do not wish to look any further.

Neither religions nor the countless reports of personal experiences, which from time immemorial may have helped to establish all religions and in modern times also helped significantly to establish esotericism, do not help us here because they often ignore the scientific aspects completely, or at least regularly, if they do not comply with preconceived notions.

And yet, all these fields of experience could help us here und the inclusion of all of them is even very important in finding the truth. However, if I talk about finding the truth, then I reject simultaneously and unambiguously all those voices which claim that such a truth does not exist. But it does indeed exist, that is absolutely certain, however, *we* will never be able to find it. This does not mean that we could not get closer to it. It depends on us to get closer to it or to move further away. We can approach this one truth through reason, logic, far-sightedness and a clear view as well as by removing our blinkers and by developing a general but not uncritical openness on all sides.

Each single field of knowledge, each religion and a great wealth of experience can give us valuable indications and aids for finding possibly more conclusive answers. Nevertheless, no single area alone will provide us with the decisive impetus for a sustainable direction in our search for this one truth and convince us of it.

Always and everywhere the interpretations provided are either dominated by a restrictive lopsidedness or an arbitrary universalism.

Clearly for me, only elementary-mathematical logic provides us with the decisive and really viable "red thread" and it is imperative that we utilise this to search for the truth. Only this logic provides us with the information which can already be found in ancient teachings.

Ignorance of reality causes some people to claim that this cannot be true, since the basic rules of mathematics are ultimately human inventions. This can easily be refuted, however, and is only the result of a lack of expertise.

1) Elementary mathematical logic *proves* that always and everywhere in this world, which we can perceive with our senses, there must be *two laterally reversed and opposing realities* (polar symmetry). This means that both entities exist in reality and do not come from nowhere. The nonentity, symbolised with the number 0, is only an axis of symmetry. These two realities are mirror images of each other. One of them is the first to develop and remains the "stronger reality". The other in turn emanates from it. Thus the latter always contains parts of the first reality. The first reality or "real existence" contains all negative numbers, the second, subsequent "real existence" all positive numbers.

The negative (natural) numbers start with −1 and extend endlessly to −eternity, the positive natural numbers start with +1 and extend endlessly to +eternity.

Since in the spatial universe, due to special considerations not to be elucidated here, it is always the squares of the natural numbers that are relevant, we can logically deduce that *each one* of these two real existences also contains parts of the other (cf. extensive explanations in my numerous books since 1999: among others *"Plädoyer für ein Leben nach dem Tod und eine etwas andere Sicht der Welt"*, 1999, not translated yet; *"A Better History of Our World" Volume 1, "The Universe", 2001; "To Perceive the World with Logic" 2007; "Nobody Ever Dies!" 2005,* and all German editions*).*

Probably more than two and a half thousand years ago the famous symbol of Yin and Yang, which to my mind has never been surpassed for conciseness and simplicity, was devised by ancient Chinese philosophers, presumably to depict exactly these interrelations.

2) Elementary mathematical logic *proves* that this "polar symmetry" is reproduced and recurs continually on every level of real existence. And if something in this world runs cyclically, i.e. it emerges, develops and eventually perishes again like all physical matter, then there is parallel to it something else which always runs linearly, i.e. it evolves and continues to grow. This applies to every spirit or, generally speaking, for all information. If, on the other hand, any physical matter also contains some information, then anything spiritual also contains some physical matter. And in the same way as the spiritual aspect grows in the physical matter, the physical texture or the physical part decreases simultaneously.

But not only that: all information progresses infinitely as mathematics *proves* exemplarily by means of those two number sequences mentioned under point 1). Each number, no matter how high, can be followed by another number.

Physical bodies generated by information, however, are finite and are never conceivable in infinite numbers. Nevertheless, they can potentially contain an infinite amount of information (for example with and within our brains). The German physician *Wilhelm Olbers (1758-1840)* pointed this out about 200 years ago, even though he drew the wrong conclusion with regard to the extension of our universe; this, however, is not the subject of this presentation (cf. my books *"Plädoyer für ein Leben nach dem Tod und eine etwas andere Sicht der Welt"*, 1999, not translated yet; *"A Better History of Our World" volume 1, "The Universe", 2001; "To Perceive the World with Logic" 2007).*

3) Elementary mathematical logic thus suggests the *convincing conclusion* that the reality of an exclusively physical world, which most of us experience, can only be one side of reality: for many religious people this sounds trivial; they believe in the spiritual element within humans, they "recognise" it. However, "modern scientists" have no interest in this since they continue to search for a (physical) "substrate" for the spiritual which does not exist. With this perception, however, they distance themselves from the "red thread" of mathematics which shows us two inversely opposed real existences. This can only mean that in opposition to our "physical world of particles" a completely other world must exist which does not consist of particles in the same manner. It follows that our hitherto valid terminology is no longer sustainable.

For many people concealed, by many others, however, simply rejected – but by no means non-existent – there is a completely other world "beyond" the physical world which we perceive with our senses (all expressions for this are ill-conceived but I *chose* "beyond"). This world originally also emerged in a similar way from a very simple origin. At first slowly, then eventually in rapidly increasing speed and in leaps and bounds it develops and unfolds to ever higher complexity. This is an informational or, in simpler words, a spiritual reality or a real existence. About two and a half thousand years ago Plato postulated this plausibly and depicted it in a wonderful way in his famous "Cave Allegory" which is universally known at least in name.

4) Elementary mathematical logic *proves* that beyond these two polar-symmetrical realities (or worlds) which we can perceive more or less clearly, or which we can at least describe, there must be a third which is the compelling basis of everything that constitutes or will ever constitute our universe. From there everything emerges and every existence must have developed from there.

This "third" reality is, however, completely beyond our cognitive capacity. We can say (almost) nothing about it apart from the fact that it must exist and that on closer inspection at least some general principles must be inherent in it since we and everything around us would not and could not otherwise exist. Here again I refer to my numerous books.

From a purely mathematical point of view, this is equivalent to the "red thread" of elementary mathematical logic, the world of the so-called "imaginary numbers". They must exist, all successive sequences of numbers emerge from there but their nature is beyond all description. Put into religious words, we could speak of a "divine level" or simply of "God" as a symbol for a higher "entity", or perhaps of a "creative power". All other "limitations" and "detailed descriptions" are completely arbitrary even if some people want to believe that they are based on their "own experiences". By doing so, they create in the end only another basis for unacceptable new dogmata which are reflected especially in institutionalised religions and often lead to superfluous disputes about conflicting concepts. In fact, we do not and cannot know anything about it.

5) Elementary mathematical logic thus *proves* that at the beginning of everything there is something eternally incomprehensible and indescribable for us but which must exist in reality. Christians speak of "God". Any other terminology would be and is just as correct and simultaneously incorrect. Mathematically abstracted it is the real basis of everything: it is the world of the really existing imaginary numbers, emanating from "i". Following on from there, the first reality or real existence is generated which by many is recognised as real, by many others, however, categorically rejected, it is something which cannot really be explored but which can basically be described:
It is the aforementioned world of increasingly complex (infinite) information, mathematically depicted by the world of negative numbers. In casual words we could speak of a "spiritual world" which is subject to evolution in the same way as the world of physical finite entities which emerges with and from it later and which mathematically correlates with the world of positive numbers.

What we call "consciousness" and thereby also "infinite and eternal consciousness" thus develops in this context of spiritual evolution.

These interrelations, which I have already termed, described in detail and explained comprehensively in my earlier books decades ago.

I find it deplorable, therefore, when later authors neither look carefully enough for earlier publications and quote long existing sources nor even name them correctly. For me this is primarily the evident lack of diligence of later authors and journalistic researchers, especially since they often want to give themselves a semblance of scientific competence. Often enough long-since published theses and theories are then merely repeated, scarcely paraphrased, and, due to poor journalism, attributed to the one who can best sell himself through clever marketing.

I myself have experienced this over the last decades. One example is the subject "near-death experiences" (NDE): Though NDE became very popular due to the book *"Life after Life"* by *Raymond Moody,* its English first edition was published in 1975, which was successfully marketed worldwide; but it was the German physician *Prof. Dr. Eckart Wiesenhütter*, neurologist and head physician at the renowned Bodelschwingsche Anstalten Bethel in Bielefeld, Germany, who had already published *"Blick nach drüben"* before, the first book on NDE after World War II, unfortunately only available in German. And there already existed books about NDE before that war as well.
To work scientifically always means, however, to work also with accuracy. Sadly, this is all too often lacking.

Many renowned scientists of our times and over the last centuries have come to similar conclusions. As an example, I would like to quote *Prof. Dr. Hans-Peter Dürr*, a physicist whom I hold in high esteem but who unfortunately died in 2014:

„ *... In the subatomic quantum world there are no objects, no matter, no substances, i.e. things we can touch and recognise. There are only motions, processes, interrelations ... It is a pure information field ... It has nothing to do with mass and energy ..."* (P.M. 5-2007).

Numerous attempts to contrast and compare cosmic evolution, the evolution of all life on this earth and indeed everywhere else in this universe, where we might meet it or where we will meet it, make it very clear: in accordance with the clear mathematical parameters always and everywhere the same happens verifiably:

1) Anything physical, be it ever so small, contains information which in the course of time amalgamates into higher complexity and continues to develop just like the physical entity itself which "contains and surrounds" it. Thus ever more complex "information clusters" are generated accordingly, alongside the "physical clusters" which we know as dust, stones, rocks or later stars and planets, for example. But at the same time, the following applies: all physical matter progresses cyclically; anything informational grows linearly.

2) Informational entities are interconnected by explicit rules. Originally, they are solely of elementary mathematical nature. These rules become ever more complex in the same way as the complexity of the informational clusters grows. Due to the constant interaction between information and its "condensation", a description of the strong "interrelations between them, and hence for something we denominate in a collective term as "physical matter", there are further and even more complex structures generated at some point in time which we identify as "organic matter". This is the beginning of a new and higher form of interaction with equally new rules which now go beyond pure mathematics. "Life" is emerging and with it a completely new quality of "information clusters". They are what we generally refer to as "spirit".

In the course of any further development in this constantly interactive cooperation and thus in the course of *evolution,* as we refer to it in a collective term, ever more complex life is gradually generated, such as plants and animals and, thereby, also new and higher forms of mutual interaction between the actual spiritual core of all these beings and their sensually perceptible physicality.

Thus, for example, intelligence and ever higher forms of consciousness and later self-consciousness develop.

Here on earth, we humans are at the moment the pride of this creation, which by no means should prove quality and, as we unfortunately know nowadays, nor does it, since, as I mentioned before, everywhere and hence here also polar symmetry reigns. And thus on the spiritual level the following also applies: Bright lights cast dark shadows...

Of course, in every situation it is up to us alone to combat and minimise these shadows as far as possible.

3) Any "informational condensation", i.e. any form of initially non-living and later living matter must, in the context of its predetermined cyclical course and at some time or other inevitably approach its end. When we refer to a living being we denote this with the word "death".

However, there is this core of, and to be found in, everything in this world which is the real "divine mystery": it is our proper very own self, the informational being "within us", our personality. We now know: anything informational keeps developing straight forward and consistently linearly upwards. This is exactly what we ourselves also experience in the course of each human life. Yet, ultimately, our death can inevitably only affect our "physical shell". The true core, our personality, which has matured to ever higher complexity in the course of our whole life, will go on living without interruption. It must live on since the principles of this world dictate it. Of course, it survives its "own death". But how?

4) Of course, the "red thread" of elementary mathematics can help us here as well, and it must protect us against erroneous assumptions based on unscientific arbitrariness after having saved us from misconceptions based on scientific bias.

Elementary mathematical logic *proves* to us that during the process of generating living organisms "perfection in its highest possible diversity" is of utmost importance on both sides and on all levels; because "the numbers" always run endlessly into infinity and thus encompass any information complex, however absurd it may seem, which can then also be eliminated again.

An analysis of evolution of all life on earth shows us impressively that only very superficial observation implies that collectivity rules the world and that indeed only on the lower levels of any development if at all.

The further evolution progresses, the more clearly it individualises itself, secondarily resulting in a collective increase in the overall standard of an entire species or parts thereof due to the multiplicity and diversity of individuals.

For us humans this means irrefutably that individuals must actively progress in their own "spiritual development" and in the event of failure they must be picked up and rescued by their "fellow human beings" if necessary. Only then will there be a collective, i.e. an overall cultural progress.

It is contra-productive to develop culture in a collective and it will never yield success. Catastrophic social trends, which started about 200 years ago and culminated in the course of the 20th century, show sad evidence thereof. Unfortunately, such notions can still be found today in many minds. This is also an indication of polar symmetry in spiritual development with (potentially) dark shadows where there is bright light.

5) It follows that death cannot be the end of the spiritual development of any single individual once it has gained a foothold. Thus death is never the end of any single living being, since basically each one of them already possesses a complex spiritual core.

Every living being continues to exist beyond its own death. However, where consciousness and individual awareness have not yet been manifested they remain without individual perception and would resemble the "morphogenetic fields" which Rupert Sheldrake, the English biologist, postulated. However, where consciousness and individual awareness emerge they will never again be lost.
This means that each of us humans keeps on living consciously after our death: uninterrupted and without any restriction. The personality of each individual remains completely intact and is the basis for our ever progressing development.

6) But how can we imagine this? Based on the "red thread" of elementary mathematical logic providing us with distinct guidelines, we can observe nature and look for similarities.

In fact, we will be successful very quickly.
Nature possesses something unique which is widely spread and numerous organisms undergo this process: this phenomenon is known as *"metamorphosis"*.

This is not merely a kind of "transition" of an organism into a "related form of life". No, it is often the "transition" of an organism into something completely different and the opening up of a whole new level of existence while completely abandoning its previous form of existence. Even single cells are formed into something entirely new by an "unknown power". The former organism has utterly changed. The British wildlife filmmaker *David Malone* describes this as follows: *"A living organism pauses suddenly, seemingly to destroy itself and to restore itself as a completely new creature. I ask myself whether we are so interested in metamorphosis because we feel subconsciously that it has something to do with ourselves"* (from: „Metamorphose", arte, Franco-German TV Network, 2014).

This means that a butterfly is not just a flying caterpillar. The butterfly is something completely new and penetrates new dimensions which a caterpillar could never perceive. Any form of physical matter is lost in this metamorphosis and collects in a kind of cellular pulp. Only the information of this organism remains intact and a mysterious purely informational choreography assembles this mash into something completely new.

We have to imagine that something similar will happen to us after our death:
We will undergo a "spiritual metamorphosis": we will enter a completely new form of existence while we abandon entirely the corporeality we knew till then. Yet all attributes of our complex personality, which is our very own "complex information cluster", grown in the course of our life on earth, remain intact. The most

beautiful word for this is and remains for me "soul". This is what lives on, strives quickly to new developments and must and will stride along completely new and unknown paths.

And since the corporeality we perceive with all our senses "here" is ultimately just some kind of "stable connection of information", which I also term here as "condensation of information", we can assume, of course, that a similar "condensation of information" will continue to exist after the spiritual metamorphosis which we call death, whereby the mutual perception is maintained. People who have experienced an NDE are often deeply irritated. Only for the bereaved "here", with their "classical physical senses", they are no longer perceivable.

So, on the one hand, our death is not the end of us, quite the contrary. This reductionist notion is part of the evil in our world and leads to extremely dangerous social tendencies and the well-known me-first mentality.

On the other hand, there is *no reincarnation*. This seems to be a widespread misconception which unfortunately results in completely unacceptable social consequences in many regions on earth, just like some other delusions, often dogmatically defended, in numerous other religions in this world.

If now some people should recount the most varied experiences they claim to have witnessed and experienced in situations in which their brain spontaneously finds itself, due to an unusual condition, or into which they deliberately manoeuvred it themselves, then this could still be authentic. In many cases this can simply be explained by the fact that everything that ever was still exists.

A brain loses this not uncommon ability to perceive these things more extensively usually during childhood already. From an evolutionary point of view this is of crucial importance to us for our survival: this so-called "reduction filter function" of our brain is a simple necessity of life.

In children this function is insufficiently developed and, in some cases, it remains "underdeveloped" for the rest of their lives. In other cases this function may also be weakened by appropriate training. All this can lead to people who posses a "mediumistic aptitude".

It is by no means always possible to convey reliable information "about another world" through the brain itself even if its reduction filter is open wider and for a longer period of time. The information undergoes all too often very personal interpretations and is "modulated", mostly quite subconsciously, on its way to the outside and before being communicated. However, parts of the information could refer to another parallel existing world and thus to the current and former lives of already dead people. But there will never be any information about one's own former life, since there has never been nor will ever be one.

If in individual cases people are completely "dominated" in the course of their lives by constant exposure to such information which may be caused by a long dead person, for example, and is due to a reduction filter that has become porous – be it gradually, as the result of a chronic disease, or suddenly, as the result of an acute trauma – then that is a pathological dysfunction of this indispensable feature of their brain. With this in mind, we can probably explain some psychiatric phenomena, such as some types of schizophrenia and especially the condition of a "multiple personality".

As cosmically unique creatures, which we all are throughout our really undefinable span of life, which from our point of view "here" might even be "eternal", we all may rest assured that we lay the foundation for our further progress in our current lives.

Each one of us will eventually rely on this foundation. For each of us it will be our "karma".

This means that the individual future will certainly be more difficult for some of us than for others, depending on the style of life we have chosen "here".

The fact remains, however, that every single one of us will have to deal with it in a completely new life in a completely new form of existence and on a completely new level of existence which is still unknown to us today.

The foundation we create here is, of course, based on a simple universally valid law, the "golden rule of ethics" which says:

Do not do to others what you do not want to be done to you!

This alone determines the starting position for our new life after a metamorphosis which we will have to face at some time or other and which, entirely without justification, we call "our death"; in fact: *"Nobody Ever Dies!"*

If everyone took this rule to heart and lived accordingly we would no longer have to experience wars and serious conflicts. But everyone will be judged in reference to this rule sooner or later.

Current Books by Prof. Dr. Walter van Laack in English language:

1. Novel:

Our Key To Eternity
ISBN 978-3-936624-18-2 (SC), 308 p. (2016)
ISBN 978-3-936624-31-1, E-Book (2016)

2. Non-fiction Books

Keystones Of Our World
The Whole World Is Information
ISBN 978-3-936624-33-5 (SC), 68 p. (2016)
ISBN 978-3-936624-34-2, E-Book (2016)

To Perceive The World With Logic
ISBN 978-3-936624-08-3, Softcover (SC), 340 p. (2007)
ISBN 978-3-936624-09-0, E-Book (2008)

Nobody Ever Dies!
ISBN 978-3-936624-03-8, (SC), 272 p. (2005)
ISBN 978-3-936624-22-9, E-Book (2013)

A Better History of Our World

Vol. 1, "The Universe"
ISBN 978-3-8311-1490-0, (SC), 188 p. (2001)
Vol. 2, "Life"
ISBN 978-3-8311-2597-5, (SC), 236 p. (2002)
Vol. 3, "Death"
ISBN 978-3-936624-01-4, (SC), 276 p. (2003)

Key To Eternity
ISBN 978-3-8311-0344-7, (SC), 256 p. (2000)

3. Bilingual non-fiction "Upside-Down" Book-Series:

"Lectures&Insights – Vorträge&Einsichten"

**Dying and Death from a Scientific Point of View –
Sterben und Tod aus wissenschaftlicher Sicht**
ISBN 978-3-936624-41-0, Softcover (SC), 44 p. (2018) 5,00 €
ISBN 978-3-936624-42-7, E-book (2018)

van Laack GmbH, Aachen, Book-Publishers (HRB-Aachen 5584)

Managing Director: Prof. Dr. Walter van Laack
Board: Dr.-Ing. Dipl.-Wirt.-Ing. Alexander van Laack,
Martin van Laack, M.Sc., Prof. Dr. Walter van Laack

Roermonder Str. 312, D- 52072 Aachen
Fax: +49-3212-9319310
Web: www.vanLaack-Book.eu – www.vanLaack-Buch.de
Email: webmaster(at)van-Laack.de

Supplied by: Book-on-Demand (BoD)
In de Tarpen 42, D- 22848 Norderstedt, Fax +49-40-534335-84
Web: www.bod.de   Email: info(at)bod.de

Autor

Prof. Dr. med. Walter van Laack
Facharzt für Orthopädie & Orthopädische Chirurgie, Physikalische Therapie,
Sportmedizin, Chirotherapie und Akupunktur,
Hochschullehrer, Buchautor, Verleger

Umschlag

Gestaltet von meinem Sohn Martin van Laack, M.A.
Master of Science in Architektur (RWTH-Aachen)

Übersetzung

von Anneliese Wolstenholme, D-Roetgen

© 2018 by **Prof. Dr. Walter van Laack**
van Laack Buchverlag, D-Aachen
www.vanLaack-Buch.de   -   www.van-Laack.de
www.Nahtoderfahrung.info

Druck & Vertrieb durch Books-on-Demand (BoD)
In de Tarpen 42, D- 22848 Norderstedt; Fax +49-40-53433584
info@bod.de   -   www.bod.de

ISBN 978-3-936624-41-0

Walter van Laack

Vorträge & Einsichten

Sterben und Tod aus wissenschaftlicher Sicht

Sterben und Tod aus wissenschaftlicher Sicht

Nach einem Vortrag von Prof. Dr. med. Walter van Laack, gehalten am 2. Juni 2018 in Fulda

Schon die berühmten Philosophen Sokrates und Platon gingen davon aus, dass unser Tod nicht auch zugleich unser Ende sein muss. Vielmehr hielten beide ein Überleben dieser für uns scheinbar undurchsichtigen Grenze für sehr wahrscheinlich. Sie waren sich aber – wie zweitausend Jahre später besonders Immanuel Kant – auch darin einig, dass weder durch persönliche Erfahrungen, noch durch Religionen oder die Philosophie allein zuverlässige Antworten auf diese Frage gegeben werden können. Allenfalls können sie mit einigen beachtenswerten und manchmal vielleicht sogar durchaus überzeugenden Hinweisen aufwarten.

Um jedoch der Wahrheitsfindung möglichst näher zu kommen, sind naturwissenschaftliche Erkenntnisse, darunter natürlich auch medizinische, heute absolut unabdingbar. Sie allein und nur für sich betrachtet führen aber auch wieder in die Irre, sofern man nicht gezielt nach einer die Tellerränder übergreifenden, ganzheitlichen Betrachtung strebt und dabei konsequent den sprichwörtlichen „Roten Faden" sucht, der als Richtschnur geeignet sein könnte und einen bei aller Phantasie und Philosophie immer wieder auf den „rechten Weg" zurückführen sollte.

Doch gibt es diesen „Roten Faden" überhaupt? Ich meine ja und versuche, das einmal mehr auch in diesem Vortrag nachhaltig und überzeugend darzulegen.

Es ist eine Tatsache, dass keine wissenschaftliche Erkenntnis, keine Messung und keine Beobachtung völlig deutungslos im Raum verharrt. Alles und jedes unterliegt zumeist sehr schnell einer Deutung oder Interpretation. Nur allzu oft wird sie aber für sich allein und ohne Einbezug womöglich paralleler Phänomene und Beobachtungen in anderen Wissens- und Erkenntnisbereichen vorgenommen. Darauf nimmt immer auch der aktuelle Zeitgeist Einfluss, der heute nach wie vor leider *materialistischer* Natur ist und damit alle Deutungen auch auf diese Basis reduziert. Deshalb spricht man auch von *Reduktionismus*. Und daher gilt aus wissenschaftlicher und medizinischer Sicht derzeit immer noch klar und kompromisslos die von den meisten Medien bevorzugte und kritiklos, weil ahnungslos verbreitete Feststellung: *Unser Tod ist das definitive Ende unserer Persönlichkeit.* Oder, wie es der in diesem Jahr verstorbene, allerorts so hoch gelobte englische Physiker *Steven Hawking* einmal vor ein paar Jahren in einem Interview äußerte: *„Ich sehe das Gehirn als einen Computer, der irgendwann nicht mehr läuft. Es gibt keinen Himmel, kein Leben nach dem Tod für kaputte Computer"* (aus „Welt am Sonntag", 22.05.2011).

Auf der anderen Seite gibt es jedoch unzählige Erfahrungsberichte von sehr vielen Menschen auf der Erde – und das wohl nicht erst heute, sondern schon seit Anbeginn der Menschheit – in denen alle möglichen Visionen und Darstellungen gleich zu einer riesigen Fülle und Vielfalt von sehr verschiedenen und sich nicht selten auch widersprechenden Möglichkeiten führen könnten, wie das, was wir unseren Tod nennen, schließlich doch überlebt werden sollte.

Natürlich ist dabei immer unglaublich viel Phantasie im Spiel, gleichwohl in nicht wenigen Fällen gepaart mit uns durchaus zu denken gebenden, verifizierbaren Erfahrungen und Erlebnissen.

Dazu gehören zum Beispiel solche während einer sogenannten Nahtoderfahrung (NTE), die jemand irgendwo an einem Unfallort oder auf einem OP-Tisch liegend hat, während er bewusstlos ist und wiederbelebt wird. Manchmal entpuppt sich das Wahrgenommene später als richtig. Nur hätte diese Erfahrung in der extremen und

lebensbedrohlichen Situation eigentlich gar nicht gemacht werden können; denn sie lag, wie wir sagen, in diesem besonderen Moment außerhalb des jeweiligen Erfahrungs- oder Erkenntnishorizontes.

Dazu gehören aber auch Erlebnisse, die jemand während bestimmter Wachheitszustände macht: In Trancen oder unter Hypnosen scheinen manchmal Menschen nicht nur frühere Situationen ihres Lebens nachzuerleben, die ihrem jetzigen Bewusstsein verborgen sind oder vielleicht auch verdrängt werden. In einigen Fällen berichten sie scheinbar auch von Erfahrungen aus früheren Leben. Manchmal sprechen sie dabei sogar eine fremde Sprache, die sie selbst nie gelernt haben, sich dann aber als korrekt erweisen mag.

In den meisten Fällen lassen sich solche Berichte anschließend nicht auf ihre Richtigkeit prüfen. Dann muss man derartige Visionen oder Erzählungen aus wissenschaftlicher Sicht als reine Anekdoten verbuchen. Das heißt deshalb jedoch nicht, dass an ihnen nichts dran ist: Nur wissenschaftlich betrachtet sind sie nicht verwertbar. Das gilt für alle ähnlichen Fälle, d.h. zum einen für solche aus der großen Gruppe spontaner „Außergewöhnlicher Bewusstseinserfahrungen" (ABE), zu denen auch die Nahtoderfahrungen (NTE) als kleine, aber sehr eindrucksvolle Untergruppe gehören. Zum anderen gilt das natürlich auch für solche, die unter Hypnosen von einem womöglich früheren Leben berichten. Gerade solche Visionen und Erlebnisse werden jedoch gerne als wahre Geschichten aus einem eigenen „früheren Leben" eingeordnet. Das aktuelle Leben wird dann als „fleischliche Wiedergeburt" interpretiert. Hierfür wurde erstmals im Jahr 1857 der Begriff *„Reinkarnation"* von dem französischen Spiritisten *Allan Kardec (1804-1861)* eingeführt.
Zahlreiche Hypnosetherapeuten bieten auf dieser Basis heute sogenannte „Rückführungen" (Regressionen) unter Hypnose an. Zahlreiche weitere Forscher glauben, mit zumeist kindlichen Visionen und Berichten aus verifizierbaren Lebenssituationen einer bereits verstorbenen Person den Glauben an derartige Reinkarnationen wissenschaftlich beweiskräftig stützen zu können.

Im Grunde treffen hier also zwei vollkommen gegensätzliche Vorstellungswelten aufeinander: Die eine Seite zieht sich aufgrund ihrer scheinbar „streng wissenschaftlichen" Sichtweise in das Schneckenhaus eines sprichwörtlichen *Einerleis* zurück. Damit betrachten sie jedoch nach meinem Dafürhalten die Welt viel zu einseitig und deshalb reduktionistisch, d.h. rein materialistisch. Auf der anderen Seite tummeln sich dafür Unzählige, die sich nur auf ihre eigenen Erfahrungsschätze oder die anderer berufen, weil sie ihnen, aus welchen Gründen auch immer, stärkeres Gewicht zumessen wollen als wissenschaftlicher Erkenntnis.

Oft führt das zu einem kaum überschaubaren und nur schwer einzuordnenden, recht beliebigen *Allerlei*. Darin vereinigen sich wohl viele Anhänger aus allen institutionalisierten Religionen sowie aus der ganzen Bandbreite der sogenannten Esoterik. Bestenfalls leben diese Gruppen nebeneinander her, zwar oft mit viel gegenseitiger Missachtung, aber wenigstens friedlich. Manchmal, und derzeit leider in wachsendem Maße, steigern sich einige solcher Gruppen zu nicht akzeptablen, oft leider sogar gewalttätigen Auseinandersetzungen, wie zurzeit gerade das Vorgehen sehr vieler religiöser Fanatiker immer wieder leidvoll zeigt.

Eine Umfrage in unserem Land von Januar 2017 unter Personen über 18 Jahren verdeutlicht das Vorhergesagte: Etwa die Hälfte der erwachsenen Deutschen glaubt weder an Seele, Gott, Leben nach dem Tod, Auferstehung von den Toten, Wiedergeburt u.s.w., während die andere Hälfte aber genau das macht, jedoch stark aufgesplittert auf die verschiedensten Vorstellungen. Frauen sind, wie diese Umfrage auch zeigt, deutlich „gläubiger" als Männer, die sogar zu etwa ⅔ alles „Spirituelle" ablehnen *(Statista 2018, 1020 Teilnehmer)*.

Dem „klassischen Wissenschaftler" muss man vorhalten, dass er seine Augen selbst dann verschließt, wenn eigentlich Unerklärliches *nachgewiesen*, wenngleich nicht wie im Labor reproduziert werden kann. Dann wird es meist einfach ignoriert oder phantasievoll interpretiert oder man verweist darauf, auch das heute noch

Unerklärliche irgendwann in der Zukunft doch reduktionistisch erklären zu können. Die modernen Ergebnisse im Rahmen der Nahtodforschung, sowohl experimentell beim Tier, als auch bei meist zufällig erfolgten zeitnahen Messungen am sterbenden Menschen, zeigen genau das: Man versucht regelmäßig, jede „Krümmung" so gerade zu biegen, dass sie doch wieder in den gewohnten reduktionistischen Rahmen zu passen scheint. Selbst für ziemlich hanebüchene und abgehobene Interpretationen ist man sich dann oft nicht zu schade.

Mit Religionsfanatikern ist dagegen leider meist kaum zu reden. Das erwächst sich dann in manchen Fällen zu einem schweren gesellschaftlichen Problem. Nur durch kompetente Politiker, von denen es heute leider mal wieder weniger zu geben scheint, könnte dies mit Vernunft und Weitsicht über geeignete Gesetze und pragmatische Rechtsprechung gelöst werden.

Dem Esoteriker muss man dagegen immer wieder nahelegen, sich mehr mit „echter Wissenschaft" zu befassen. Notorisch wird vieles durch seine einmal ausgerichtete Brille betrachtet, wobei er nicht selten sogar glaubt, diese Sichtweise sei wissenschaftlich untermauert. Dem ist aber oft nicht so. Meine Erfahrung der letzten Jahrzehnte ist leider die: Sehr oft steht auch hier pure Dogmatik im Vordergrund und vorgefasste Meinungen variieren mit großer Variation und Bandbreite, jedoch ohne wirkliche Substanz.

Nach jahrzehntelanger Forschung und intensiver Beschäftigung mit dem Thema Tod, der Frage nach seiner Endgültigkeit und den dazu gängigen Antworten aus allen beteiligten Wissenschaften bin ich zu folgenden Feststellungen gekommen:
Die klassischen Wissenschaften helfen uns nicht immer wirklich weiter, weil man sich dort meist nur mit den Phänomenen der eigenen Fachgebiete beschäftigt und kaum über den eigenen Tellerrand blickt und oft auch gar nicht blicken möchte.
Weder die Religionen, noch die unzähligen Erfahrungsberichte, die ursprünglich wohl seit alters her alle Religionen und heutzutage auch

die Esoterik im Wesentlichen mitbegründen, helfen uns hier immer wirklich weiter, weil sie das Wissenschaftliche oft ganz, zumindest aber dann regelmäßig außen vor lassen, wenn es nicht zu vorgefertigten Ansichten passt.

Dabei könnten uns alle Bereiche weiterhelfen und die Hinzuziehung aller ist sogar zur Wahrheitsfindung sehr wichtig. Wenn ich allerdings von Wahrheitsfindung spreche, dann weise ich in demselben Atemzug und unmissverständlich all jene Stimmen zurück, die meinen, eine solche Wahrheit gäbe es gar nicht. Oh doch, es gibt sie, ganz sicher sogar, nur werden *wir* sie nie finden können. Das heißt aber nicht, dass wir uns ihr nicht nähern könnten. Es liegt an uns, sich ihr zu nähern oder weiter zu entfernen. Nähern können wir uns dieser einen Wahrheit durch Vernunft, Logik, Weitsicht und Übersicht sowie durch das Ablegen von Scheuklappen und mit Entfaltung einer grundsätzlichen, aber nicht unkritischen Offenheit nach allen Seiten.

Jedes Wissensgebiet, jede Religion und viele Erfahrungsschätze können uns dabei wertvolle Hinweise und Hilfen für dann vermutlich schlüssigere Antworten geben. Gleichwohl wird uns kein einziges Gebiet allein die entscheidenden Impulse für eine tragfähige Richtung auf der Suche nach dieser einen Wahrheit liefern und uns überzeugen können.

Immer und überall dominieren entweder eine beengende Einseitigkeit in der Betrachtung oder eine beliebige Vielseitigkeit in Bezug auf die angebotenen Interpretationen.

Für mich eindeutig liefert uns nur elementare mathematische Logik den entscheidenden „Roten Faden", den wir als wirkliche Hilfe auf der Suche nach Wahrheit zwingend benötigen. Nur sie liefert uns Hinweise, die wir zum Teil sogar schon in alten Lehren finden.

In Unkenntnis der Realität behaupten manche, dies könne nicht stimmen, weil auch die Grundregeln der Mathematik letztlich menschliche Erfindungen seien. Das aber ist eindeutig zu widerlegen und bloß das Ergebnis mangelnden Sachverstands.

1) Elementare mathematische Logik *beweist,* dass es immer und überall in dieser von uns sinnlich wahrnehmbaren Welt *zwei spiegelbildliche und gegensätzliche Realitäten* geben muss (polare Symmetrie). Beide existieren also real und kommen nicht aus dem Nichts. Das Nichts, symbolisiert durch die Zahl 0, ist bloß eine Symmetrieachse. Beide Realitäten verhalten sich spiegelbildlich zueinander. Eine von beiden entsteht als erste und ist auch die „stärkere Realität". Die andere entspringt wiederum aus ihr. So enthält Letztere immer auch einen Teil der ersten Realität. Die erste Realität oder „reale Existenz" umfasst alle negativen Zahlen, die zweite, ihr nachfolgende „reale Existenz", dagegen alle positiven.

Die negativen (natürlichen) Zahlen beginnen mit −1 und gehen endlos bis −Unendlich, die positiven natürlichen Zahlen beginnen mit +1 und reichen endlos bis +Unendlich.

Da aufgrund spezieller, hier nicht weiter zu vertiefender Überlegungen, im räumlichen Universum immer die Quadrate der natürlichen Zahlen maßgeblich sind, kann daraus logisch gefolgert werden, dass *jede* dieser beiden realen Existenzen auch einen Teil der anderen in sich trägt (vgl. ausführliche Erläuterungen in zahlreichen meiner Bücher seit 1999: unter anderem in *„Plädoyer für ein Leben nach dem Tod und eine etwas andere Sicht der Welt",* 1999; *„Eine bessere Geschichte unserer Welt",* Bd. 1, *„Das Universum",* 2000; *„Mit Logik die Welt begreifen,"* 2005; *„Wer stirbt, ist nicht tot!",* 2003 und 2011, sowie alle englischen Versionen).

Vermutlich schon vor mehr als zweieinhalbtausend Jahren entstand genau hierfür in der alten chinesischen Philosophie das berühmte und in meinen Augen durch nichts besser, prägnanter und einfacher darstellbare Symbol von Yin und Yang.

2) Elementare mathematische Logik *beweist,* dass sich diese „polare Symmetrie" auf jeder Ebene der Realexistenz stets aufs Neue ergibt und wiederfindet. Und wenn etwas in dieser Welt stets zyklisch verläuft, also entsteht, sich entwickelt und irgendwann wieder vergeht wie etwa alles Materielle, dann gibt es dazu parallel auch etwas anderes, das immer linear verläuft, also sich bildet und

immer weiter wächst. Dies gilt für alles Geistige oder, ganz allgemein, für alle Information. Wenn andererseits jedem materiellen Etwas auch etwas Informationelles innewohnt, dann haftet auch jedem geistigen Etwas wieder etwas Materielles an. Und so wie das Geistige im Körperlichen wächst, nimmt zugleich die materielle „Konsistenz", bzw. der materielle Anteil ab.

Aber nicht nur das: Alles Informationelle, so *beweist* uns die Mathematik beispielhaft anhand der beiden unter 1) vorgenannten Zahlenreihen, läuft endlos weiter. Jeder noch so hohen Zahl ließe sich eine weitere anfügen.

Aus Information sich bildende materielle Körper sind dagegen endlich und auch niemals in unendlicher Zahl denkbar. Gleichwohl können sie potentiell unendlich viele Informationen beinhalten (zum Beispiel mit und in unseren Gehirnen). Dies hatte schon der deutsche Arzt *Wilhelm Olbers (1758-1840)* vor etwa 200 Jahren erkannt, wenngleich er daraus einen falschen Schluss für die Ausdehnung des Universums gezogen hatte, was aber nicht Gegenstand dieses Beitrags ist (siehe dazu meine Bücher *„Plädoyer für ein Leben nach dem Tod und eine etwas andere Sicht der Welt", 1999; „Eine bessere Geschichte unserer Welt", Bd. 1, „Das Universum", 2000; „Mit Logik die Welt begreifen", 2005).*

3) Elementare mathematische Logik legt somit *beweiskräftig* den Schluss nahe, dass die von den meisten von uns wahrgenommene Realität einer ausschließlich materiellen Welt nur die eine Seite der Wirklichkeit sein kann: Für viele religiöse Menschen ist das trivial; denn sie glauben ja an das Geistige in sich, sie „erkennen" es. Die „moderne Wissenschaft" kann damit jedoch nichts anfangen, weil sie nach einem (materiellen) „Substrat" für das Geistige sucht, das es nicht gibt. Mit dieser Vorstellung entfernt sie sich allerdings von dem „Roten Faden" der Mathematik; denn die lehrt uns zwei spiegelbildlich-gegensätzliche reale Existenzen. Das aber heißt zwingend, dass unserer „materiellen Teilchenwelt" eine ganz andere Welt gegenüberstehen muss, die *nicht in derselben Weise* aus

Teilchen besteht. Damit aber sind auch unsere bisher gültigen Begrifflichkeiten nicht mehr haltbar.

Für viele verborgen, von vielen anderen wiederum einfach abgelehnt – aber deshalb keineswegs nicht-existent – befindet sich „hinter“ der von uns *mit unseren Sinnen wahrgenommenen*, materiellen Welt (alle Ausdrücke dafür sind schlecht, ich *wähle* halt „hinter“) eine vollkommen andere Welt. Auch sie entsteht ursprünglich einmal in derselben Weise aus dem ganz Einfachen. Zunächst allmählich, dann irgendwann schnell zunehmend und sprunghaft, entwickelt und entfaltet sie sich zu immer höherer Komplexität. Hierbei handelt es sich um eine informationelle oder, einfacher gesagt, eine geistige Realität oder reale Existenz. Schon vor zweieinhalbtausend Jahren wurde sie von Platon in seinem berühmten und allseits zumindest dem Namen nach bekannten Höhlengleichnis plausibel gefordert und in wundervoller Weise dargestellt.

4) Elementare mathematische Logik *beweist*, dass es hinter den beiden von uns mehr oder weniger deutlich wahrnehmbaren, zumindest aber beschreibbaren, polar-symmetrischen Realitäten (oder Welten) noch eine dritte geben muss, die allem, was dieses Universum ausmacht und jemals ausmachen wird, zwingend zugrunde liegt. Aus ihr entsteht all das überhaupt erst, und alles, was ist, muss aus ihr entstanden sein.

Diese „dritte“ Realität entzieht sich jedoch völlig unserer Erkenntnisfähigkeit. Zu ihr können wir (fast) nichts sagen, außer dass es sie zwingend geben muss und dass ihr bei näherer Betrachtung zumindest ein paar allgemeine Grundsätze zu Eigen sein dürften, da es uns und alles um uns herum sonst nicht so gäbe und geben könnte. Auch hier verweise ich auf meine zahlreichen Bücher.

Rein mathematisch betrachtet handelt es sich hierbei entsprechend dem „Roten Faden“ elementarer mathematischer Logik um die Welt der sogenannten „imaginären Zahlen“. Es muss sie geben, aus ihr lassen sich sukzessiv alle Zahlenreihen bilden, aber ihr Wesen entzieht sich jeglicher Beschreibung. Religiös formuliert könnten wir

hier von „Göttlicher Ebene" oder einfach von „Gott" als Symbol für eine höhere „Einheit" sprechen, vielleicht auch gut von einer „Schöpfungsmacht". Alle weiteren „Eingrenzungen" und „näheren Beschreibungen" sind völlig willkürlich, auch wenn manche sie auf „eigenen Erfahrungen" gestützt glauben wollen. Damit aber bilden sie am Ende nur wieder die Basis für neue unzulässige Dogmen, die sich gerade auch in institutionalisierten Religionen widerspiegeln und leider oft zu überflüssigen Auseinandersetzungen gegensätzlicher Auffassungen führen. Tatsächlich wissen wir dazu nichts und können es auch nicht.

5) Elementare mathematische Logik *beweist* somit, dass am Anfang von allem etwas steht, das für uns ewig unbegreiflich und unbeschreiblich ist, aber real existieren muss. Christen sprechen von „Gott". Jede andere Begrifflichkeit wäre und ist genauso richtig und falsch zugleich. Mathematisch abstrahiert ist es eine reale Basis von allem: Es ist die Welt der real-existenten imaginären Zahlen, ausgehend von „i". Daraus entsteht zunächst die durchaus von vielen als real erkannte, von vielen anderen dagegen kategorisch abgelehnte, weil nicht mit unseren Sinnen wahrnehmbare und somit nur wenig wirklich erforschbare, dennoch aber grundsätzlich beschreibbare, erste Realität oder reale Existenz:

Es ist die schon erwähnte Welt der sich zu immer höherer Komplexität entwickelnden (unendlichen) Information, mathematisch dargestellt durch die Welt der negativen Zahlen. Salopp gesagt können wir von einer „Geistigen Welt" sprechen, die genauso einer Evolution unterliegt, wie die sich erst mit ihr und aus ihr danach entwickelnde Welt der materiellen, endlichen Körper, die mathematisch der Welt der positiven Zahlen entspricht.

Im Rahmen der geistigen Evolution entsteht so auch das, was wir „Bewusstsein", und damit auch „endloses und ewiges Bewusstsein" nennen. Diese Zusammenhänge habe ich schon vor Jahrzehnten in früheren Büchern so benannt, detailliert beschrieben und umfassend erläutert.

Ich finde es daher bedauerlich, und für mich ist es vor allem ein Zeugnis mangelnder Sorgfalt sowohl späterer Buchautoren als auch journalistischer Rechercheure, ganz besonders, da sie sich zumeist den Anstrich wissenschaftlicher Kompetenz geben wollen, wenn sie zum einen nicht umsichtig genug nach früheren Veröffentlichungen Ausschau halten und längst vorhandene Quellen zitieren und zum anderen wenigstens korrekterweise benennen. Oft werden dann längst publizierte Thesen oder Theorien mit kaum anderen Formulierungen bloß wiederholt und infolge schlechten Journalismus dem zugeschrieben, der sich durch geschicktes Marketing am besten verkaufen kann.

Ich habe das in den letzten Jahrzehnten selbst erfahren müssen. Dazu ein Beispiel zum Thema „Nahtoderfahrungen" (NTE): Zwar wurden NTE sehr populär durch das weltweit erfolgreich am Markt platzierte Buch *„Leben nach dem Tod"* von *Raymond Moody* und der englischen Erstausgabe *„Life after Life"* im Jahr 1975. Es war aber der deutsche Arzt *Prof. Dr. Eckart Wiesenhütter*, Neurologe und Chefarzt der renommierten Bodelschwingschen Anstalten Bethel in Bielefeld, der bereits zuvor mit *„Blick nach drüben"* das erste Buch der Nachkriegszeit zu NTE veröffentlich hatte, jedoch nur in Deutsch. Und auch vorher gabe es bereits Bücher zu dieser Thematik. Wissenschaftlichkeit bedeutet aber immer auch Genauigkeit. Daran mangelt es jedoch leider allzu oft.

Viele große Wissenschaftler unserer Zeit und in den letzten jahrhunderten kamen schon zu ähnlichen Schlüssen. Beispielhaft möchte ich dazu den 2014 verstorbenen, von mir sehr geschätzten Physiker *Prof. Dr. Hans-Peter Dürr* zitieren:

„ ... In der subatomaren Quantenwelt gibt es keine Gegenstände, keine Materie, keine Substanzen, also Dinge, die wir anfassen und begreifen können. Es gibt nur Bewegungen, Prozesse, Verbindungen, Informationen ... Es ist ein reines Informationsfeld ... Es hat nichts zu tun mit Masse und Energie ..." (P.M. 5-2007).

Eine Vielzahl von Gegenüberstellungen und Vergleichen im Rahmen der kosmischen Evolution, der Evolution allen Lebens auf dieser Erde

und sicher auch sonst überall in diesem Universum, wo wir darauf noch treffen könnten und vielleicht sogar noch werden, macht sehr deutlich: Entsprechend den klaren mathematischen Vorgaben existiert immer und überall nachprüfbar dasselbe:

1) Jedem noch so kleinen materiellen Etwas haftet Information an, die sich im Laufe der Zeiten genauso zu immer größerer Komplexität zusammenschließt und fortentwickelt wie das „sie beherbergende, äußere" materielle Etwas selbst auch. So entstehen neben „materiellen Clustern", die wir zum Beispiel als Staub, Steine, Felsen oder später Sterne und Planeten kennen, entsprechend auch immer komplexere „Informationscluster". Aber zugleich gilt: Alles Materielle nimmt zyklische Verläufe, alles Informationelle wächst linear.

2) Information ist durch klare Regeln miteinander verbunden. Sie sind ursprünglich allein elementar-mathematischer Natur. Auch diese Regeln werden immer komplexer, so wie die Komplexität der informationellen Cluster wächst. Irgendwann kommt der Zeitpunkt, da bilden sich im steten Zusammenspiel zwischen Information und ihrer „Kondensation" als Bezeichnung für die stabilen „Beziehungen zwischen ihnen" und damit für das, was wir dann per Sammelbegriff als „Materie" bezeichnen, weitere und noch komplexere Strukturen heraus, die wir als „organische Materie" bezeichnen. Damit beginnt eine neue und höhere Form des Zusammenwirkens mit ebenso neuen, nun auch über die reine Mathematik hinausgehenden Regeln. Es entsteht „Leben" und mit ihm eine ganz neue Qualität der „Informationscluster". Sie nennen wir nun ganz allgemein „Geist".

Im Laufe jeder weiteren Entwicklung dieses stets interaktiven Zusammenspiels und damit im Laufe dessen, was wir als Ganzes *Evolution* nennen, entsteht allmählich auch immer komplexeres Leben, entstehen zum Beispiel Pflanzen und Tiere, und damit auch wieder neue und höheren Formen der gegenseitigen Beeinflussung zwischen dem eigentlichen *geistigen* Kern all dieser Wesen und ihrer sinnlich wahrnehmbaren Körperlichkeit.

So entwickeln sich zum Beispiel Intelligenz und immer höhere Formen von Bewusstsein und später (Selbst-)Bewusstheit.

Hier auf dieser Erde sind wir Menschen zurzeit die Krone dieser Schöpfung, was aber keineswegs einen Qualitätsbeweis darstellen muss und, wie wir heute leider wissen, auch nicht darstellt; denn wie ich schon sagte, überall und so auch hier regiert polare Symmetrie. Und damit gilt auf geistiger Ebene genauso: Wo viel Licht, da leider auch viel Schatten…

Natürlich liegt es in jeder Situation allein an uns, diese Schatten zu bekämpfen und möglichst zu minimieren.

3) Jede „informationelle Kondensation", also jede Form von zunächst noch nicht lebender und später dann lebender Materie, muss im Rahmen seines vorbestimmten zyklischen Verlaufs irgendwann einmal zwangsläufig seinem Ende entgegenstreben. Das bezeichnen wir beim lebenden Wesen dann mit dem Wort „Tod".

Doch da gibt es ja diesen Kern von und in allem in dieser Welt, der das eigentliche „göttliche Geheimnis" ist: Es ist unser eigentliches „Ich", das informationelle Wesen „in uns", unsere Persönlichkeit. Wir wissen nun: Alles Informationelle entwickelt sich schnurstracks und konsequent linear aufwärts weiter. Genau das erleben wir auch an uns selbst im Laufe eines jeden menschlichen Lebens. Damit jedoch kann unser Tod schließlich zwangsläufig nur unsere „materielle Hülle" betreffen. Der eigentliche Kern, unsere über unser ganzes Leben zu immer größerer Komplexität herangereifte Persönlichkeit, lebt dagegen ohne Zäsur weiter. Sie muss weiterleben, weil es die Gesetze dieser Welt erfordern. Sie überlebt natürlich den „eigenen Tod". Aber wie?

4) Selbstverständlich kann uns der „Rote Faden" elementarer Mathematik auch hier weiterhelfen und muss uns, nachdem er uns vor der sicher falschen Vorstellung unseres endgültigen Todes als Folge wissenschaftlicher Einseitigkeit bewahrte, nun ebenso vor irrigen Annahmen aufgrund unwissenschaftlicher Beliebigkeit schützen.

Elementare mathematische Logik *beweist* uns, dass auf beiden Seiten und allen Ebenen der Existenzwerdung grundsätzlich „Perfektion in größtmöglicher Vielfalt (Vielheit)" angesagt ist; denn

„die Zahlen" laufen stets endlos ins Unendliche und beinhalten damit jeden auch noch so abstrusen Informationskomplex, der folglich aber auch wieder ausgemerzt werden kann.

Eine Untersuchung der Evolution allen Lebens auf unserer Erde zeigt uns eindrucksvoll, dass nur bei sehr oberflächlicher Betrachtung Kollektivität die Welt regiert und das auch allenfalls auf den unteren Ebenen jeder Entwicklung.

Je weiter die Evolution voranschreitet, desto klarer individualisiert sie sich, wobei es dann sekundär, über die Vielheit und Vielfalt der Individuen, wieder zu einem auch kollektiven Anheben des Gesamtniveaus der ganzen Art oder Teilen davon kommt.

Auf uns Menschen übertragen heißt das ohne Wenn und Aber: Jeder Einzelne muss aktiv mit seiner eigenen „geistigen Entwicklung" voranschreiten und bei seinem Versagen notfalls durch „den Nächsten" aufgefangen und mitgenommen werden. Erst dann kommt es zu einem kollektiven, d.h. einem gesamtkulturellen Fortschritt.

Kultur über das Kollektiv zu entwickeln ist kontraproduktiv und wird nie zum Erfolg führen. Katastrophale gesellschaftliche Strömungen, beginnend im 19. Jahrhundert und bislang kulminierend im 20., bieten dafür unzählige traurige Beweise. Leider finden sich derartige Vorstellungen selbst heute noch in so vielen Köpfen. Auch das ist ein Zeichen von polarer Symmetrie der geistigen Entwicklung mit (potentiell) viel Schatten wo viel Licht.

5) Der Tod kann also nicht das Ende der geistigen Entwicklung eines jeden sein, wenn diese bereits einmal Fuß gefasst hat. Und damit ist der Tod niemals das Ende von irgendeinem Lebewesen, da ja jedes grundsätzlich schon einen komplexen geistigen Kern besitzt.

Jedes lebende Wesen existiert über den eigenen Tod hinaus weiter. Dort aber, wo Bewusstsein und eigene Bewusstheit noch nicht manifestiert sind, bleibt es ohne individuelle Wahrnehmung und würde zu der Vorstellung von „Morphogenetischen Feldern" des englischen Biologen Rupert Sheldrake passen. Dort aber, wo Bewusstsein und individuelle Bewusstheit hervortreten, werden

diese niemals mehr verloren gehen. Damit lebt jeder von uns Menschen nach seinem Tod bewusst weiter: ohne Zäsur und ohne jede Einschränkung. Die Persönlichkeit eines jeden bleibt vollends erhalten und ist die Basis für seine immer weiter fortschreitende Entwicklung.

6) Wie aber kann man sich diese dann vorstellen? Da uns der „Rote Faden" elementar-mathematischer Logik klare Richtungen vorgibt, können wir auf dieser Grundlage nun in die Natur schauen und nach Ähnlichem suchen. Tatsächlich werden wir sehr schnell fündig.

In der Natur gibt es etwas Einzigartiges, das weit verbreitet ist und von zahllosen Lebewesen durchlaufen wird: Es ist bekannt als das Phänomen der *„Metamorphose"*.

Hierbei handelt es sich nicht nur um eine Art „Übergang" eines Wesens in eine „verwandte Lebensform". Nein, oft handelt es sich um den „Übergang" eines Wesens in etwas *völlig anderes* mit Erschließung einer ganz neuen Exstenzebene und unter völliger Aufgabe dessen, was seine bisherige Existenzform ausmachte.
Sogar einzelne Zellen werden dabei von einer „unbekannten Macht" zu etwas Neuem geformt. Das ehemalige Wesen hat sich vollständig verwandelt. Der britische Naturfilmemacher *David Malone* beschreibt das so: *„Ein Lebewesen hält plötzlich inne, um sich scheinbar selbst zu zerstören und als vollkommen neues Geschöpf wiederherzustellen. Ich frage mich, ob wir uns so sehr für die Metamorphose interessieren, weil wir unterbewusst spüren, dass sie auch etwas mit uns selbst zu tun hat"* (aus: „Metamorphose", arte – TV, 2014).

So ist ein Schmetterling nicht nur eine fliegende Raupe. Mit ihm ist etwas völlig Neues entstanden und dringt jetzt in eine ganz andere, für eine Raupe niemals erkennbare Dimension ein. Alles Materielle geht bei dieser Metamorphose der Form nach verloren und sammelt sich in einer Art Zellbrei. Nur die Information des Wesens bleibt erhalten und fügt diesen Brei durch eine geheimnisvolle, rein informationelle Choreographie zu etwas völlig Neuem neu zusammen.

So ähnlich müssen auch wir uns wohl das vorstellen, was uns nach unserem Tod erwartet:

Wir vollziehen eine „geistige Metamorphose": Es ist der Eintritt in eine ganz andere und völlig neue Existenzform, unter kompletter Aufgabe dessen, was wir bis dahin an Körperlichen an uns kannten. Doch bleiben dabei sämtliche Attribute unserer komplexen Persönlichkeit, die unser eigener, im Laufe unseres hiesigen Lebens gewachsener, „komplexer Informationscluster" ist, erhalten.

Das schönste Wort hierfür ist und bleibt für mich das Wort „Seele". Genau das ist es, was weiter lebt, flugs auf zu neuen Entwicklungen strebt und dabei auf völlig neuen und unbekannten Wegen schreiten muss und wird.

Und da auch alle mit unseren Sinnen „hier" wahrgenommene Körperlichkeit letztlich bloß eine Art „informationell gesteuerte, stabile Verbindung von Information" ist, die ich hier einfach als „Kondensation von Information" bezeichne, können wir natürlich davon ausgehen, dass eine ähnliche „Kondensation von Information" nach dieser geistigen Metamorphose, die wir den Tod nennen, weiterbesteht, womit die gegenseitige Wahrnehmung erhalten bleibt. NTEler sind durch diese Erfahrung, die sie häufig machen, zutiefst irritiert. Allein für die Hinterbliebenen „hier" ist man so nicht mehr mit ihren ja „klassisch materiellen Sinnen" wahrnehmbar.

Somit ist einerseits unser Tod nicht unser Ende, ganz im Gegenteil. Diese reduktionistische Vorstellung ist ein Teil des Übels unserer Welt und führt leider zu äußerst gefährlichen Gesellschaftstendenzen und dem bekannten Ellbogendenken.

Andererseits gibt es aber auch *keine Reinkarnation*. Diese scheint mir genauso ein sehr verbreiteter Irrglaube zu sein, der in vielen Regionen dieser Erde leider völlig untragbare gesellschaftliche Konsequenzen nach sich zieht, wie natürlich auch einige andere, oft sehr dogmatisch verfochtene Fehlvorstellungen in zahlreichen anderen Religionen dieser Welt.

Wenn nun manch einer in Situationen, in denen sich sein Gehirn spontan befinden kann oder in die man es sogar vorsätzlich

hineinmanövriert, von den unterschiedlichsten Dingen erzählt, die er dabei erfahren und erlebt haben will, so kann das dennoch richtig sein. Es ist in vielen Fällen einfach damit zu erklären, dass all das ja noch nach wie vor weiter existiert, sofern es einmal war.

Die durchaus nicht seltene Fähigkeit, solche Dinge vielleicht sogar umfangreicher wahrzunehmen, verliert ein Gehirn normalerweise schon in der Kindheit. Das ist evolutionär betrachtet für jeden von uns von ausschlaggebender Bedeutung, und zwar um zu überleben: Diese sogenannte „Reduktionsfilterfunktion" des Gehirns ist eine schlichte Lebensnotwenigkeit.

Bei Kindern ist dieser Filter oft noch nicht ausreichend entwickelt, bei manchen bleibt er sogar ein Leben lang „unterentwickelt". Bei wieder anderen lässt er sich womöglich auch durch geeignetes Training abschwächen, so dass „mehr Informationen" durchkommen. All das kann zu „medial begabten Menschen" führen.

Keineswegs lassen aber sich durch das Gehirn selbst bei längerer und größerer Öffnung seines Reduktionsfilters Informationen „von einer anderen Welt" immer auch zuverlässig übermitteln. Nur allzu oft werden sie auf dem „Weg nach draußen", also bis zu dem Moment, wo sie kommuniziert werden, zumeist ganz unbewusst sehr persönlichen Deutungen unterworfen und „moduliert". Dennoch können sich darunter solche aus einer anderen, zu der unsrigen parallel existenten Welt finden, und damit auch aus der aktuellen und früheren Lebenswelt von bereits verstorbenen Menschen. Niemals aber sind es Informationen aus einem eigenen, früheren Leben; denn das gab und gibt es nicht.

Wenn dann in Einzelfällen jemand durch die ständige Einwirkung solcher Informationen aufgrund eines – allmählich durch chronische Krankheit oder plötzlich als Folge eines akuten Traumas – porös gewordenen Reduktionsfilters in seinem weiteren Leben sogar regelrecht „beherrscht" wird, zum Beispiel durch eine tatsächlich längst verstorbene andere Person, dann handelt es sich um eine pathologische Entgleisung dieser lebensnotwendigen Einrichtung

unseres Gehirns. Damit lässt sich womöglich manches in der Psychiatrie erklären, so wie etwa Formen der Schizophrenie und speziell das Krankheitsbild einer „Multiplen Persönlichkeit".

Als ein kosmisch einzigartiges Wesen, welches jeder von uns zeit seines heute nicht näher eingrenzbaren, aus unserer Sicht vielleicht „ewigen" Lebenswegs ist, dürfen wir jedoch alle getrost davon ausgehen, dass wir in diesem aktuellen Leben das Fundament für unseren weiteren Werdegang legen.

Auf diesem baut jeder von uns einmal auf. Für jeden von uns wird es zu seinem „Karma".

Damit aber wird es der eine zukünftig ganz bestimmt einmal schwerer haben als der andere, je nachdem, wie man sein eigenes Leben „hier" gestaltet hat.

Immer aber wird jeder Einzelne in einem ganz neuen Leben in einer ganz neuen Existenzform und auf einer ganz neuen und heute für uns noch unbekannten Existenzebene damit fertig werden müssen.

Das Fundament, das wir alle hier begründen, fußt natürlich auch wieder auf einem einfachen, für jeden universell gültigen Gesetz, der „Goldenen Regel der Ethik", die lautet:

Was du nicht willst, das man dir tu, das füg auch keinem anderen zu!

Dies allein bestimmt unsere Startposition für unser neues Leben nach unserer irgendwann bevorstehenden Metamorphose, die wir völlig zu Unrecht „unseren Tod" nennen; denn tatsächlich gilt:

„Wer stirbt, ist nicht tot!"

Würde jeder diese Regel für sich berücksichtigen, gäbe es schon hier keinerlei Kriege und keine ernsthaften Auseinandersetzungen mehr. Daran aber wird jeder dereinst gemessen werden.

Aktuelle Bücher von Prof. Dr. Walter van Laack in deutscher Sprache:

1. Roman:

Unser Schlüssel zur Ewigkeit
ISBN 978-3-936624-16-8, Taschenbuch (SC), 316 S. (2015), 18,00 €
ISBN 978-3-936624-27-4, E-Book (2015)

2. Sachbücher

Mit Logik die Welt begreifen
ISBN 978-3-936624-04-5, Taschenbuch (SC), 380 S., (2005), 29,80 €
ISBN 978-3-936624-07-6, Festeinband (HC), 380 S. (2005), 39,80 €
ISBN 978-3-936624-23-6, E-Book (2013)

Wer stirbt, ist nicht tot!
ISBN 978-3-936624-12-0, (SC), 272 S., (Neuauflage 2011), 24,80 €
ISBN 978-3-936624-13-7, (HC), 272 S., (Neuauflage 2011), 35,00 €
ISBN 978-3-936624-21-2, E-Book (2013)

Eine bessere Geschichte unserer Welt

Band 1, "Das Universum"
ISBN 978-3-8311-0345-4, (SC), 196 S. (2000), 15,80 €

Band 2, "Das Leben"
ISBN 978-3-8311-2114-4, (SC), 248 S., (2001), 17,80 €

Band 3, "Der Tod"
ISBN 978-3-8311-3581-3, (SC), 276 S., (2002), 19,80 €

Der Schlüssel zur Ewigkeit
ISBN 978-3-9805239-4-3, (HC), 288 S.,1. Aufl. (1999), 24,80 €
ISBN 978-3-89811-819-4, (SC) , 288 S., 2. Aufl.. (2000), 17,80 €

**Plädoyer für ein Leben nach dem Tod
und eine etwas andere Sicht der Welt**
ISBN 978-3-89811-818-7; (SC), 448 S., 2. Aufl. (1999/2000), 22,90 €

3. Bilinguale „Upside-Down"-Sachbuchreihe: Vorträge&Einsichten – Lectures&Insights

Sterben und Tod aus wissenschaftlicher Sicht – Dying and Death from a Scientific Point of View
ISBN 978-3-36624-41-0, Taschenbuch (SC), 44 S. (2018), 5,00 €
ISBN 978-3-936624-42-7, E-Book (2018)

4. Tagungsbände

Schnittstelle Tod – Sind Religionen religiös und Wissenschaften wissend?
ISBN 978-3-936624-36-6, Taschenbuch (SC), 172 S. (2018), 18 €

Schnittstelle Tod – Wo stehen wir nach 40 Jahren NTE-Forschung?
ISBN 978-3-936624-30-4, Taschenbuch (SC), 92 S., (2016), 14,00 €
ISBN 978-3-936624-32-8, E-Book (2016)

Schnittstelle Tod – Was spricht für unser Weiterleben?
ISBN 978-3-936624-19-9, Taschenbuch (SC), 100 S., (2014), 14,00 €

Schnittstelle Tod – Warum auf ein Danach vertrauen?
ISBN 978-3-936624-14-4, Taschenbuch (SC), 120 S., (2012),15,00 €

Schnittstelle Tod – Aufbruch zu neuem Leben?
ISBN 978-3-936624-10-6, Taschenbuch (SC), 148 S., (2010), 19,80 €

van Laack GmbH, Aachen, Buchverlag
(HRB-Aachen 5584)

Geschäftsführer: Prof. Dr. Walter van Laack
Gesellschafter:
Dr.-Ing. Dipl.-Wirt.-Ing. Alexander van Laack,
Martin van Laack, M.Sc., Prof. Dr. med. Walter van Laack

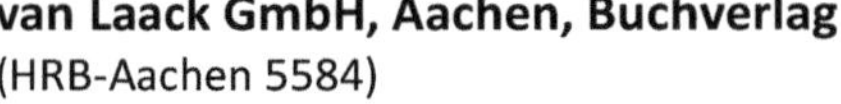

Roermonder Str. 312, 52072 Aachen
Fax: 03212-9319310
Web: www.vanLaack-Buch.de   www.Nahtoderfahrung.info
Email: webmaster(at)van-Laack.de

Vertrieb durch: BoD, Book-on-Demand
In de Tarpen 42, 22848 Norderstedt – Fax 040-534335-84
Web: www.bod.de – Email: info(at)bod.de